FACING LIFE'S CHALLENGES

FACING DISCRIMINATION

BY GOLRIZ GOLKAR

BLUE OWL BOOKS

TIPS FOR CAREGIVERS

Social and emotional learning (SEL) helps children manage emotions, create and achieve goals, maintain relationships, learn how to feel empathy, and make good decisions. The SEL approach will help children establish positive habits in communication, cooperation, and decision-making. By incorporating SEL in early reading, children will be better equipped to build confidence and foster positive peer networks.

BEFORE READING

Talk to the reader about discrimination. Explain how discrimination is hurtful and prevents some people from enjoying the same rights as others.

Discuss: Have you ever experienced discrimination? Have you ever seen this happen to someone else? How did you react? Do you think this was the best way to respond?

AFTER READING

Talk to the reader about how people can work together to end discrimination. Talk about ways to promote diversity and kindness at school and in your community.

Discuss: What are some ways you can help people feel more equal in the community? Can you think of ways to help your classmates feel more included?

SEL GOAL

Children who experience discrimination may feel anxiety, anger, and other negative emotions. Ask them to write down ideas for managing their feelings in a healthy way. Help them come up with new ideas, such as mindfulness exercises, athletic activities, or art projects. Talk about how these activities can help release tension and help the reader feel joy.

TABLE OF CONTENTS

CHAPTER 1

WHAT IS DISCRIMINATION?

Justin is deaf. He signs. When he moved to a new school, no one else knew **sign language**. Justin felt left out. He had trouble learning.

He and his parents asked for help. Now an **interpreter** helps him. He learns easily with his class. His classmates even learned some signs!

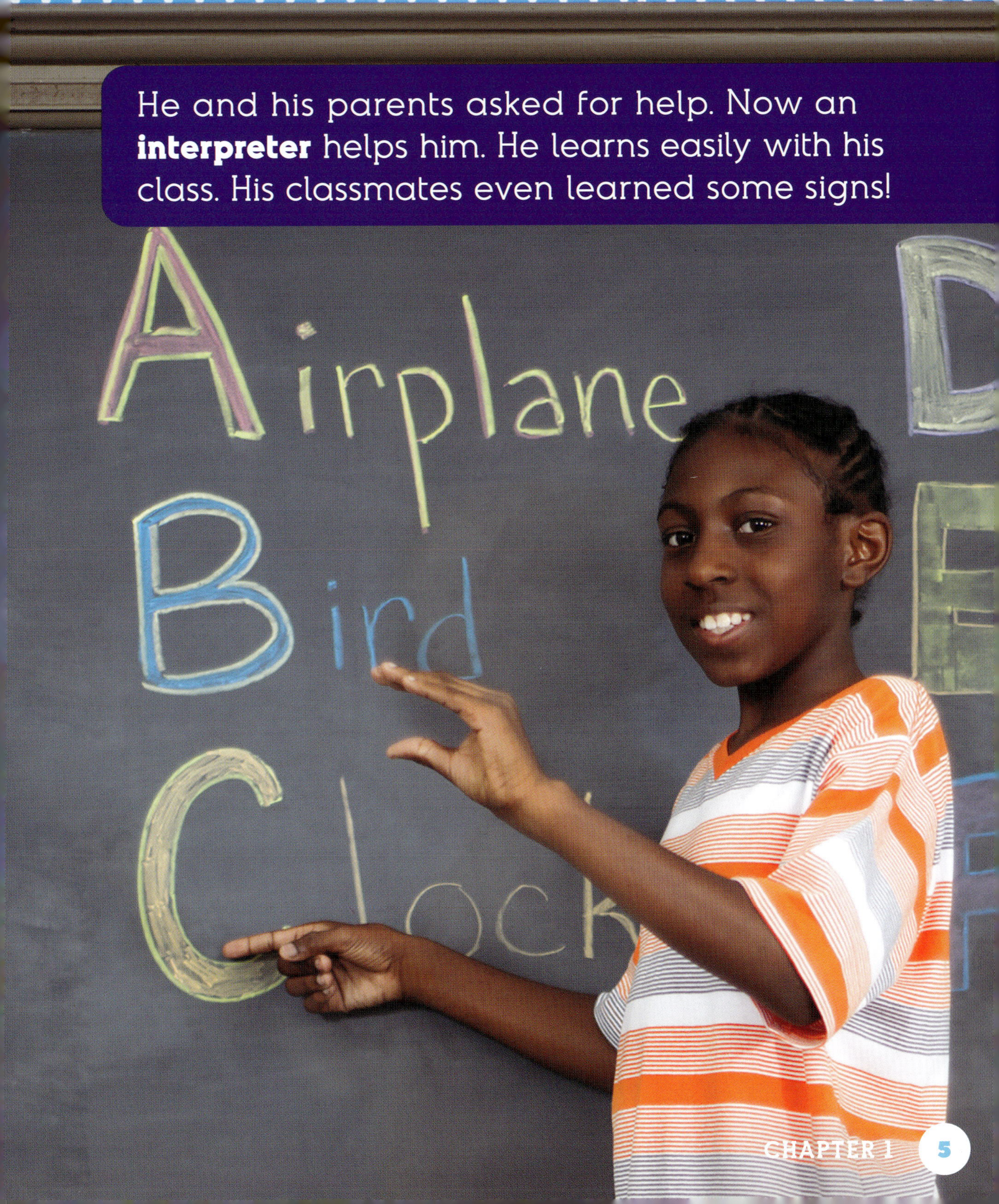

Some people are treated unfairly because of their differences. This is discrimination.

People may discriminate against **race**, religion, or **ethnicity**. They may also discriminate against age, **gender**, **disability**, or **appearance**. Sometimes, unfair rules discriminate against certain groups.

LAWS TO PROTECT

In the United States, laws protect people from discrimination when getting a job or finding a home.

Discrimination can make you feel **anxious**, sad, angry, and scared. It might stop you from doing activities you enjoy. You may have trouble **focusing** or speaking up at school.

IT'S OK TO WALK AWAY

If discrimination makes you feel unsafe, calmly walk away. Never fight back. Ask a trusted adult for help right away.

CHAPTER 2

SPEAKING UP FOR YOURSELF

Lily has two dads. Some classmates made fun of her family drawing. They said she should have a mom and a dad. This upset Lily. She talked to her teacher about her feelings.

Her teacher asked the class to talk about their families. Some kids had one parent. One boy had two moms. Two kids were adopted. The class learned that all families are special!

Lily experienced **direct discrimination**. She was treated differently from everyone else. If this happens to you, take a deep breath. Keep calm. Tell the person who is making you uncomfortable to stop. Tell them mean comments hurt. Your differences make you who you are.

Discrimination can hurt your **confidence**. It can also make you feel upset and confused. You may feel like you don't belong. Ask a trusted adult for help. He or she can help you think of what to say to someone who hurt you.

SHARE YOUR FEELINGS

Talk to your friends about your feelings. They can listen and help you feel better. Continue talking with trusted adults about your feelings and anything you may still need help with.

CHAPTER 3

HELPING OTHERS

Rita and Luis speak Spanish and English. Their public library only had books in English. This is **indirect discrimination**. In this case, unfair rules affect people who share certain **traits**.

Rita and Luis asked the librarian to help them. Their friends asked, too. Now the library has books in Spanish and other languages!

You may notice discrimination in your community. Maybe some buildings only have steps to get inside. People who use wheelchairs, strollers, and canes cannot climb them. You can ask an adult to help you reach out to the city or building owners to make a change.

ASK FOR HELP

Ask friends and family to speak up, too. Discrimination can be stopped if people speak up together. Rules can be changed. More people will feel included.

Discrimination is wrong and hurtful. Speak up for yourself and for others. Listen to everyone's feelings. Ask teachers at school to plan more activities that celebrate **diversity**.

When we talk about our differences, we can better understand each other. We can make sure we treat everyone fairly and equally.

GOALS AND TOOLS

GROW WITH GOALS

Seeing or experiencing discrimination can be upsetting. Try these goals to help you process your emotions.

Goal: Make a list of the different kinds of discrimination you have experienced or seen.

Goal: Think about how discrimination makes you feel. Ask your family and friends how it makes them feel. Have they ever experienced it?

Goal: With your family or friends, discuss ways to manage your feelings when you see or experience discrimination. Together, think of steps you can all take to stop discrimination.

TRY THIS!

You may see examples of discrimination in your community. Ask your friends and family to help you speak up about it.

- Describe examples of discrimination in your community to your friends and family. Tell them how you think it could be stopped. Ask them for other examples they have noticed.
- Write a letter to your city's mayor or to any business that could help stop the discrimination.
- Ask your friends and family to add details to your letter and sign it. You can ask other community members to sign it, too. Give your letter to the person or business you have written to and ask for a response.

GLOSSARY

anxious
Worried or very eager to do something.

appearance
The way something or someone looks.

confidence
A belief that you have the necessary ability to succeed.

direct discrimination
Treating someone unfairly because of a particular trait of that person.

disability
A physical, mental, cognitive, or developmental condition that can limit a person's ability to do certain tasks.

diversity
The condition or fact of being different.

ethnicity
A social group that shares a common culture, religion, or language.

focusing
Concentrating on something.

gender
The state of being male or female.

indirect discrimination
Unfair rules or policies that are the same for everyone but especially affect a particular group of people.

interpreter
A person who translates for people who speak or communicate using different languages.

race
One of the major groups into which humans can be divided. People of the same race share similar physical characteristics, which are passed from one generation to the next.

sign language
A system of hand movements used for communication, especially by people who are deaf.

traits
Qualities or characteristics that make people different from each other.

TO LEARN MORE

Finding more information is as easy as 1, 2, 3.

1. Go to www.factsurfer.com
2. Enter "**facingdiscrimination**" into the search box.
3. Choose your book to see a list of websites.

INDEX

Blue Owl Books are published by Jump!, 5357 Penn Avenue South, Minneapolis, MN 55419, www.jumplibrary.com

Library of Congress Cataloging-in-Publication Data

Names: Golkar, Golriz, author.
Title: Facing discrimination / Golriz Golkar.
Description: Minneapolis, MN: Jump!, Inc., [2023] | Series: Facing life's challenges | Includes index. | Audience: Ages 7–10
Identifiers: LCCN 2021053776 (print)
LCCN 2021053777 (ebook)
ISBN 9781636908106 (hardcover)
ISBN 9781636908113 (paperback)
ISBN 9781636908120 (ebook)
Subjects: LCSH: Discrimination—Juvenile literature. | Prejudices—Juvenile literature. | Equality—Juvenile literature.
Classification: LCC HM821 .G66 2023 (print)
LCC HM821 (ebook) | DDC 305—dc23/eng/20211104
LC record available at https://lccn.loc.gov/2021053776
LC ebook record available at https://lccn.loc.gov/2021053777

Editor: Eliza Leahy
Designer: Molly Ballanger

Photo Credits: RapidEye/iStock, cover (left); Dragon Images/Shutterstock, cover (right); Kamira/Shutterstock, 1; Maskot/Getty, 3; Littlekidmoment/Shutterstock, 4; huePhotography/iStock, 5; fotosparrow/Shutterstock, 6–7 (background); Ann Gaysorn/Shutterstock, 6–7 (foreground); adriaticfoto/Shutterstock, 8–9; Oksana Mizina/Shutterstock, 10; kali9/iStock, 11, 20–21; SDI Productions/iStock, 12–13; xavierarnau/iStock, 14–15; PeopleImages/iStock, 16; Jeffrey Isaac Greenberg 7+/Alamy, 17; powerofforever/iStock, 18–19.

Printed in the United States of America at Corporate Graphics in North Mankato, Minnesota.